Garfield
LARD OF THE JUNGLE

BY JIM DAVIS

Ballantine Books ● New York

Published in the United States by Ballantine Books, an imprint of The Random House Publishing Group,
a division of Random House, Inc., New York.

BALLANTINE and colophon are registered trademarks of Random House, Inc.

ISBN 978-0-345-52584-0

Printed in the United States of America

www.ballantinebooks.com

9 8 7 6 5 4

HI, JON, IT'S LIZ. I CAN'T DECIDE WHAT TO WEAR TONIGHT

AT FIRST I THOUGHT MY BLUE DRESS WOULD BE PERFECT, BUT THEN I DECIDED MY RED TOP AND SKIRT WOULD LOOK EVEN BETTER...

THEN I COULDN'T FIND ANY SHOES TO GO WITH **THAT**, SO I SWITCHED TO THE GREEN COCKTAIL DRESS, BUT THE ZIPPER ON THAT WAS STUCK...

SO I TRIED THE PURPLE STRAPLESS GOWN ON, BUT THE CLUTCH PURSE THAT GOES WITH IT HAS A HUGE MASCARA SMUDGE ON IT, AND BESIDES, I STILL THINK IT MAKES MY HIPS LOOK BIG...

SO NOW I'M BACK TO THE DRESS, UNLESS I CAN FIND A WAY TO MAKE THAT RED TOP AND SKIRT WORK WITH SANDALS, OR SOMETHING OPEN-TOED IN A NEUTRAL COLOR

JIM DAVIS 5-25

WHAT ARE YOU WEARING?

MY SUIT

HURRAY FOR GUYS

17

www.garfield.com

JIM DAVIS 7-6

JIM DAVIS 7-13

77

Distributed by Universal Press Syndicate

JIM DAVIS 10-19

I AM A NEW STATE-OF-THE-ART MULTIFUNCTION DIAGNOSTIC SCALE

I NOT ONLY PROVIDE DIGITAL AND VOICE WEIGHT MEASUREMENT TO THE TEN-THOUSANDTH OF A POUND...

BUT ALSO BODY FAT PERCENTAGE, A MUSCLE MASS INDEX RATING, PULSE READING, BODY TEMPERATURE...

...OXYGEN, BLOOD PRESSURE, AND BLOOD SUGAR LEVELS, HDL AND LDL COUNTS, AND EKG MEASUREMENTS

PLEASE STEP ON

JIM DAVIS 11-16

GREAT GOOGLY MOOGLY!

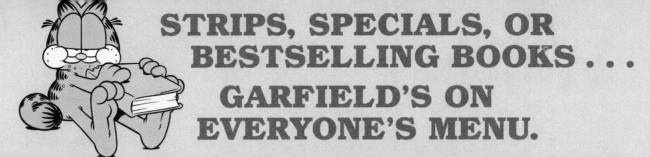

STRIPS, SPECIALS, OR BESTSELLING BOOKS . . . GARFIELD'S ON EVERYONE'S MENU.

Don't miss even one episode in the Tubby Tabby's hilarious series!

New larger, full-color format!